MW00487794

Tic-Tac-Toe of Life:

THE NOW, OWN, AND WON ANOINTING

Dr. Curtis Keith Minter

TRILOGY CHRISTIAN PUBLISHERS

TUSTIN, CA

Trilogy Christian Publishers
A Wholly Owned Subsidary of Trinity Broadcasting Network
2442 Michelle Drive
Tustin, CA 92780

Copyright © 2020 by Dr. Curtis Keith Minter

All Scripture quotations, unless otherwise noted, taken from THE HOLY BIBLE, NEW INTERNATIONAL VERSION®, NIV® Copyright © 1973, 1978, 1984, 2011 by Biblica, Inc.® Used by permission. All rights reserved worldwide.

Scripture quotations marked (KJV) taken from The Holy Bible, King James Version. Cambridge Edition: 1769.

All rights reserved, including the right to reproduce this book or portions thereof in any form whatsoever.

For information, address Trilogy Christian Publishing

Rights Department, 2442 Michelle Drive, Tustin, Ca 92780.

Trilogy Christian Publishing/ TBN and colophon are trademarks of Trinity Broadcasting Network.

For information about special discounts for bulk purchases, please contact Trilogy Christian Publishing.

Manufactured in the United States of America

Trilogy Disclaimer: The views and content expressed in this book are those of the author and may not necessarily reflect the views and doctrine of Trilogy Christian Publishing or the Trinity Broadcasting Network.

10 9 8 7 6 5 4 3 2 1

Library of Congress Cataloging-in-Publication Data is available.

ISBN 978-1-64773-889-1

ISBN 978-1-64773-890-7 (ebook)

Contents

About the Author

Dr. Curtis Keith Minter, Evangelist

Curtis Minter is the founder of Real Life International Mission, Inc., a Georgia based non-profit evangelistic organization that was established in September of 1999. He was born in Marietta, Georgia, but relocated to Douglasville, Georgia, and is married to a beautiful woman of God, Bobbie Jean Minter. Curtis is known for his strong anointing with young people. After accepting Jesus Christ at the age of twelve, Curtis served in the ministry by working with children and the youth on church bus routes, in Sunday school, in youth groups, and in children's church. At the age of sixty-two, he has been in ministry for fifty years and has seen thousands come to know Jesus Christ. He has taken over thirty mission trips in the past thirty years, traveling to Jamaica, the Bahamas, Haiti, Trinidad, Zimbabwe, and Nigeria, and to many cities in the United States like Anchorage and New Orleans. Curtis has an overwhelming passion to reach the lost and to empower people from all walks of life.

He is known for his phenomenal and revelatory gift through the Holy Spirit called Power-In-Names ("PIN"), doing spiritual name analysis using the gifts of prophecy and word of knowledge for the Body of Christ. PIN is an evangelistic tool for the lost and helps believers with their identity. He and his wife have the ability to enrich the lives of people by showing them the power in their God-given name. They are active doing the PIN teaching on the One Love Gospel Cruise, Cruise With

A Cause, home gatherings, churches, men's, women's, and youth conferences, and even at worldly events to be a light to the world. Bobbie and Curtis have been foster parents going on eight years, having twelve kids over the seven-year span. The Minters, as of 2020, have adopted three boys who are brothers, adding to their family Jayden, Devon, and Marcel. Curtis has forty-five-plus years refereeing/umpiring/officiating football, wrestling, lacrosse, and softball.

Curtis is an active member of Word of Faith Family Worship Cathedral, under the leadership of Bishop Dale C. Bronner. He has served in many ministries like GAP, KFC, CEO, RISE, and Voices of Light. Curtis attended Baptist University of America and is the recipient of many community and civic honors. He received an Honorary Doctorate in Theology from Muskegon Christian University in 2009. He, along with his wife Bobbie, hosted a successful and thought-provoking television program called Real Life Today, and Curtis and his wife were guests many times on different radio stations, here locally and abroad. At their home in Douglasville, Curtis has built "The Minter Adventure Land," with two ziplines coming off the tree fort, along with hiking trails, an eighteen-hole putt-putt course, swing sets, sand boxes, a tramline, a man tower, a twenty-one-foot screen where they have backyard movies and kick and hit baseballs, soccer balls, golf balls—any kind of balls—into the screen, and much more. Curtis Minter is a humorous, passionate, and unique man who is sold out for the cause of Jesus Christ.

Dedication

I would like to dedicate this book to my Lord and
Savior Jesus Christ; my wife Bobbie Minter, for be-

lieving in me and being a true helpmeet; my daughter Monica Meacham-Minter; my dad Harold Minter; my mother Shirley Minter (transitioned to heaven); my twin brothers Derek and Eric Minter; and my sister Lynne Yates. I must also mention Natalie Fuller, Beverly Barracks, Elaine Griffin, and Tomyko Levi; Pastor Fred Jones, Sr.; my Bishop and Pastor Dale C. Bronner; Rev. Charles Blackshear; Emmanuel Williams; Darrell Spearman; and my Word of Faith Family Worship Cathedral church family. I would like to thank the Trilogy and TBN Team for publishing my book. I want to include all of my twelve foster children and my three adopted children—Jayden, Devon, and Marcel Minter—and the rest of my friends whom I love so much.

Foreword

The history of three-in-a-row can be traced back to ancient Egypt, where such game boards have been found on roofing tiles dating from around 1300 BC. An early variation of **tic-tac-toe** was played in the Roman Empire around the first century BC, but even with all its simplicity, the history is richer and more surprising than you'd think. In the Roman era, their version was admittedly much more difficult than the one we know today. Each player used three pebbles, and so had to move around on each turn to keep playing to fill the empty spaces. So, what is your favorite memory of X's and O's?

I felt led to write the foreword my **own** book—not being proud or haughty, but grateful. You know, God is awesome to the highest degree. This book has been written for years, sitting in my computer for such a time as this. As you look around and see all that is going on, where are the handwritten notes? In families, sitting all together at dinnertime has faded away for many households. We are so busy with Facebook, chat lines, texting, dating apps, and the list goes on. With technology and social media, are we missing something? What happened to kids being able to run to the neighbor's without concern? To people really helping each other and watching out for our best interests? I remember a time when I would not think twice about picking up a hitchhiker. Times have really changed, and writing this book has changed me—and I am sure it will change you. So, move forward; let the words of this book inspire you inside and out. This book will help you reestablish your **NOW** and fix an outline of your **OWN**—a new way of control in carrying your plans out. It will teach you the finishing grace of your understanding, showing you that you have **WON**. The teams have been working hard—they have practiced long and hard, and now it's game time. That is you; you are in the locker room, ready to come out.

The coach comes over to you and announces that you are ready, and that he has placed you on the starting lineup. Something rises in you—a confidence that you can do it. Then, you take a deep breath and rise to your feet, and it's all history after that. The butterflies go away after the first play is done. The **NOW**, **OWN**, and **WON** has started its process.

Watch these 3 Letters change your life ...

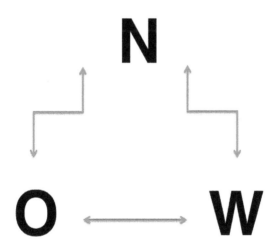

Interchangeable   NOW - OWN - WON

CHAPTER 1

Introduction

Tic-Tac-Toe, three in a row. Wherever you are in life, let's create three in a row. God has always worked in threes. For example: we have the sun, the moon, and the stars; we have breakfast, lunch, and dinner; and we have the Father, the Son, and the Holy Spirit. God made us body, soul, and spirit—three parts. We date, we get engaged, and then we get married.

The body has three parts: we have a head, a torso, and limbs.

← HEAD

TORSO →

↑
← LIMBS
(2 ARMS
& 2 LEGS)

We even have three parts to our arms, legs, and fingers.

Look at the arm:
(1) Upper arm - From the shoulder to the elbow (bicep)
(2) Forearm - From elbow to wrist
(3) Hand – With the fingers

FOREARM ↓ UPPER ARM ↓

HAND→

←THIGH

CALF →

← FOOT

(1) Thigh
(2) Calf
(3) Foot

God truly made us in His image and likeness. Even trouble and blessings sometimes come in threes. I would rather have the blessings—what about you?

So, life is full of surprises. It takes tests and troubles, problems, conflicts, and bumps in the road of life to shape and mold us. Life is a blessing in itself. Life

3

is what you make out of it. Every day is full of choices. Your age is a sum of the decisions and choices you make every day. The objective of this book is to examine where you are with your life and what it is going to take to get you where you want to be. There is a lot of talk about "going to the next level," but how do you get there? Could a word—or let's say, could three words—change your life forever? I believe they could, just like the words right below changed me.

Here they are: **NOW**, **OWN**, and **WON** are three simple words with the same letters—*just arranged differently by spelling*—giving us different meanings. When applied, it will change your life! I am sure that you need something to happen **NOW**. I am also sure that if you **OWN**ed a few more things, it would change your life. I am even more positive that if you understood that you had already **WON** in every situation, your mindset would be different. Are you ready to open the package? Time is not waiting for anybody. Let's do it together—**NOW!**

Three letters, three words: **N - - O - - W**, **O - - W - - N**, and **W - - O - - N**.

These words will change your outlook, your up-look, and your inward look. They will change you from the inside out and the outside in—like shake, rattle, and roll. If you have an open mind and want your heart to be filled with renewed thinking and different perspectives, it will happen to you. Can you say, "It's time for a total restoration"? So, let the principles of **NOW**, **OWN**, and **WON** change your life forever. I call **NOW**, **OWN**, and **WON** "power-packed" words with a secret anointing attached to them that can make you a world-changer. Get ready for the release of the anointed power to change the way you do things: **NOW**, **OWN**, and **WON**.

I believe God is moving in the "shift of suddenly" because of the last days we are in. Look at the storms, hurricanes, COVID-19, 9/11—everything from the church house to the White House. It seems things are speeding up. The things that took you ten years to do, you will be able to do in one year. The things that took you one year to do, you will be able to do in one month. The things that took you one month to do, you will be able to do in one week. The things that took you one week to do, you will be able to do in one day. The things that took you one day to do, you will be able to do in one hour. The things that took you one hour to do, you will be able to do in one minute. The things that took you one minute to do, you will be able to do in a matter of seconds. If you did not know, I just prophesied to you. Read this paragraph over and over and receive your prophetic word. The question is: Are you ready? If you are not ready—get ready! The "shifts of suddenly" are ready to speed up for you **NOW**, as you **OWN** it and realize you have **WON**.

I hear a sound of revival coming like never before. God has allowed what we would label "bad" to just get our attention back to Him. I know God has done some great things in the past, but a new season is rising up. Do you feel the wind blowing? Gates and doors that have been shut for years are opening up **NOW**. The last shall be first; you have been in line for a long time, but that's about to change. People who are faithfully serving God, the ones who are unknown at this point, will be rising to the forefront. As it is written, "The last shall be first and the first last" (Matt. 20:16 KJV). A stirring of gifts and talents is manifesting like cream rising to the top. God is up to something big for those who seek Him. Those who are seeking will see the King—it's all in the word seeking (see-the-king)—and while we are talking about season, it's also in the word season—when you (see-a-son). When you see Jesus, you know you are in your season. So, seek and see that the NOW, OWN, and WON will be a tool of anointing to help the shifting, shaking, and awakening.

Do you want to play the **Tic-Tac-Toe** of life and find the anointing of your **NOW**, your **OWN**, and your **WON**? Are you ready to move forward into your destiny? It's time for you to taste and see that the Lord is good, giving you power, purpose, identity, and destiny in life. Line it up; purpose to have three in a row, working the puzzle of your life, and do it **NOW—OWN** it, because you have **WON**. Nike says "Just Do It." Life is too short to miss out on your dreams and goals, and to watch others make it while you strike out. It's time for you to hit your home run, to fulfill your destiny. Life is good, but life can be so much better. Play the game of reality. Get ready to turn your future on by ringing the bell of the three little words loaded with power, passion, and purpose. Turn on the power of your mind, will, and emotions to find your passion, live your purpose, and stop helping everyone else live out their dreams while you are not being fulfilled. Take that step of faith **NOW**.

TAKING A STEP OF
FAITH

It's time for you to work on yourself, and these little words with the dynamite power of anointing attached will do it for you. It's your time to **OWN**. It's your turn to wake up from your dream, walk out your vision, and build your legacy, because you have **WON**. Study this book, apply the principles, and let the mysteries of God be your treasure that you will find in the pages ahead. Do it **NOW**, and **OWN** it now, because you have already **WON**. You can **OWN** it—and yes, you have already **WON**. Three simple letters, **N-O-W**; three simple words used together, just like when we were kids playing *Tic-Tac-Toe*. Let's play!

Before we go any further, let's put on the brakes that will help you see what God has taught me. The average Christian/believer or non-believer only looks at, studies, and examines things in the physical and soul realm. I wear reading glasses almost all the time, but it's like I am wearing 3D glasses, so I see everything in the third dimension. I look at things in the **body** (physical), **soul** (which is your mind, will, and emotions), and the last dimension, the **spirit**. So, I see the spiritual side in almost everything I do. It's like the noun, which is a person, a place, or a thing. Every person I see, every place I see, and everything I see, I look at it spiritually. It is also called walking in the Spirit. This is what I am calling the third dimension. That's how I believe God trained me to view words, names, objects—and the list goes on. Anybody can do it. Basically, again, it's walking in the Spirit. The Holy Spirit taught me—or I caught it, is a better way to say it—but that came after I got really big on the teaching of the **body, soul** and **spirit**. A lot of believers have not stepped into this knowledge. I said all of that to say this: you must begin to see the three dimensions of God, and you will and can do it. There again, it is simply turning on the Spirit. We know it, but it's another thing to do it. But that is what Christ teaches: to die daily to the flesh and walk in the Spirit. We must do this every hour, in every given day.

3 D   Look at God - Body, Soul and Spirit (I see it)

For example, let's look at money. In the physical (body), we need to have money to buy and sell. In the soul realm, we need to get the mind of God to acquire money. If we go make money, that's counterfeiting; we need the mind, will, and emotions to acquire money, because counterfeiting could put us in jail. So, in the physical (body), money is tangible, physical dollars. In the soul realm, we work a job or acquire a means to receive money. So, what is money in the Spirit? _____, I am glad you asked; the answer is: we are money! Yes, we are—okay, how? If Christ **OWN**s the cattle on the ten thousand hills and all belongs to Him, and He is inside us and we are in Him, that makes us **OWN** with Him—and we are joint-heirs with Christ, so we are money. You could say we are rich in Him. Our Daddy has it all, and He shares with His children. All we need is to find the account number; the deposit was done before the foundation of the world. So, all the money we need is already inside us **NOW**, because we **OWN** it through Him, so we have **WON** God's lottery. I love talking to people in line at a convenience store, buying a lottery ticket. I tell them that I hit the lottery every day; they look at me with an excited face and I say, "Yes, God's lottery—pressed down, shaken together, and overflowing into my lap."

For fun, God put numbers in the Bible, and He will give you the account number—but most folks are fighting over (my - one) "m-one-y," when it all belongs to Him. Money is a tool, but like I said, we are money. We are a walking, living bank, filled with all the resources we need; it's already inside of us **NOW**.

CORPORATE *Prayer*

Let's look at prayer; what is prayer in the physical (body)? We come together corporately and pray as one body, believing what we pray about. Then in the soul realm we try to get the mind, will, and emotions of God when we pray—or we should. So, what is prayer in the third dimension (**spirit**)? The answer is simple: we are prayer, the same as money. We are an answer to someone's prayer every day. God will place you in the right place at the right time—when? **NOW**. We are graced in our daily life, in the marketplace; we are anointed for ministry, working the Gospel of Christ to **OWN**. We are prayer, and we have **WON** to be an answer. So, I believe that with help, as you continue reading and looking at words, relationships, things, whatsoever in the third dimension, that you will catch it. I do not believe you can teach it, but I believe you can catch it. We are not created to function in one dimension, or just two dimensions, but *all* dimensions—the **body**, **soul**, and **spirit**. In the middle of "p-ray-er" is ray. Every time someone prays for you, it shines a ray of hope on you. Every time you pray, God shines a ray of hope on the one you are praying for. It's time to win; you have WON in your prayer life, so OWN it and do it NOW.

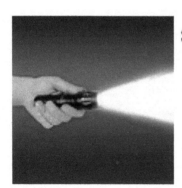

Shine a ray of

Hope

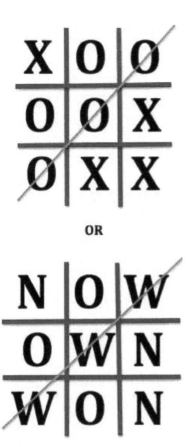

OR

So, let's put it to work right **NOW**, because when you get three in a row, you win in the **X's** and **O's**. But **NOW**, we can play and operate in the **NOW**. The **NOW** is the way you look at it. The question is, are you going to play in the third dimension? It's not the **X's** or **O's** in this game; it's the **N's**, **O's**, and **W's**. That's how you play **NOW**, **OWN**, and **WON**.

It's simple when you look at the body, soul, and spirit of the **NOW**, **OWN**, and **WON** of your life. In this book you will see and study the vision, purpose, attitude, prayer, passion, faith, peace, identity, power, victory, healing, and revival of **NOW**, **OWN**, and **WON**. Twelve principles pulled out of the **NOW**, the **OWN**, and the **WON**. Enjoy these blessings of the life-changing principles that you will unlock with the keys giving you wisdom, understanding, and knowledge; your **WUK**— your **W - W**isdom of God, your **U - U**nderstanding of God, your **K - K**nowledge of God—to move and grow in grace in the pages to come. If you have wisdom and understanding of God, and not knowledge, you are out of balance. If you have understanding and knowledge, and you do not have the wisdom of God, you are out of balance—and so forth. It's a trinity; you've got to have all three. Reminders: play *Tic-Tac-Toe* in all dimensions, because you can get three in a row with your **WUK** in *Tac*.

W - *Wisdom of God*
U - *Understanding of God*
K - *Knowledge of God*

WUK

CHAPTER 2

NOW

The NOW Factor:
Principle of Doing it NOW, with the NOW Anointing

The **NOW** factor and the principle of doing it **NOW** with the **NOW** anointing is based on Hebrews 11:1 (KJV), "**NOW** faith is the substance of things hoped for, the evidence of things not seen." We choose to operate in the NOW faith, the **NOW** anointing, the substance of things hoped for. Things that might not be ours yet, but they will be, with prayer and faith and the will of

God. It's the evidence of things not seen, but that's in the natural. We are looking in the supernatural anointing of **NOW**. **NOW** is defined as two to five seconds ago. When? **NOW**. No, that's two to five seconds ago—when? **NOW**. The **NOW** anointing is for you—when? **NOW**.

We cannot depend on yesterday's anointing, yesterday's blessing, and yesterday's opportunities. We are in the **NOW** anointing, this moment in time. Yesterday is gone! Last minute is gone! We need to work in the dimension of the **NOW**. Subdue, humble yourself under the mighty hand of God. Take dominion **NOW**; seize the day, and control every minute and second **NOW** by being God-centered, not self-centered. If you can, pack your bags and go with me into the **NOW**, and understand the power of the gracing of the **NOW** lifestyle. If you can travel to every stop along the way to digest the fullness of the total package of the **NOW**, it will be worth your while. Whatever you face in life, look at the **NOW** of it; God will strengthen you to have the confidence and wisdom to acquire every right and holy desire. Life boils down to the choices we make, so we need God to guide us in the NOW anointing.

BODY, SOUL & SPIRIT

(3) Dimensions
The Body
The Soul
The Spirit

Ready for the journey, got your bags packed? When? **NOW**! Okay, are you ready? This will be one of the best trips that you have taken in a long time. Imagine that you are about to take your seat, and over the intercom the flight attendant says, "Fasten your seatbelts." Here we go, into the dimensions of **NOW**. The **NOW** has three (3) dimensions and twelve (12) levels as we take our journey together. Get in your seat and buckle up; here we go... NOW.

BODY, SOUL & SPIRIT

The Three (3) Dimensions of NOW

3D

God made man with three parts: body, soul, and spirit. Let's look at the **NOW** in body, soul, and spirit. This is where we will find the foundations of the **NOW** anointing. I have always been *big* on the body, soul, and spirit, like I said earlier. I cannot look at objects, words, or names without seeing them in 3D—the body, the soul, and the spirit. In other words, I look at everything in the third dimension, and I want you to catch it also. I cannot teach you how to do it, but you can catch it. I believe it's the way the Holy Spirit trained me to walk in the Spirit of God, and I know you can also. I do not want to miss anything God has for me, so I take in everything in the three dimensions, and my desire is for you to acquire it for yourself. I have made it a lifestyle. The body is the physical things, the soul is our mind, will, and emotions, and the spirit is where the Holy Spirit abides. There again, we are a spirit housed in a body. I choose to function in all three (3) dimensions, the way God created us, at the same time every day, and the good thing is, you can also trust me. Allow the Holy Spirit to show you to not only walk in the Spirit but to walk in all three (3) dimensions.

Three (3) Dimensions
The Body
The Soul
The Spirit

BODY

1) The Body of NOW

The body of **NOW** is a physical reality. The body is the objects that are around us everywhere. It's time and space. If we would operate in the time and space of the **NOW**, we would be successful, taking advantage of our surroundings—called space and the element of time allotted to us. Tangible things and physical things are all around us, everywhere we choose to go and be. The buildings, the cars, the physical clothing we wear. Taking the body of the **NOW** and processing it. It is based on the decisions we make. Do we pick it up, do we carry it—and the list goes on and on as we process what to do, or do nothing at all. The dimension of the NOW is a hands-on approach, knowing what to touch and perhaps what to let go. It's the physical process that applies to every human being. Everything we see, everything we touch, has a meaning and purpose to it. Can you imagine a world without words or names? In the physical realm, the body of **NOW** is action and reaction, with a response on what to do and when to do it. God saw the darkness, and in the **NOW**, He said, "Let there be light." We are in dark situations from time to time, and we have the power through Christ to say, "Let there be light." The body of **NOW** goes to the root, and as deep as you choose. We must physically put substance together and work with what God gives us. This is the natural realm, and the spirit of **NOW** is the supernatural realm. We take our natural gifts that come from God and seek His anointing to birth them in this dimension, where we can develop it. **NOW**, in the body realm, has tangible and workable tools to increase blessings on all levels of our lives.

SOUL

(Mind - Will - Emotions)

2) The Soul of NOW

The soul of **NOW** is the mind of God, the will of God, and the emotions of God. Through this process, our mind, will, and emotions must operate in the **NOW** to stay balanced. The soul has three parts, just like the children of Israel (1) came out of Egypt; (2) went through the desert; and then (3) entered the Promised Land. We too must take the same journey. However, in order to accomplish this, we need to stop being enslaved in our minds and come out of Egypt. We must go through the process of the will of the desert, and press our emotions to get to the soul of **NOW**, the Promised Land. If we are not thinking in the soul of **NOW**, our mind, will, and emotions will play tricks on us. Focus is the key in asking the right questions, like: What is the mind of God; what is the will of God; and what is the emotion of God? All three questions must apply to the soul of **NOW**. Right **NOW**, at this very moment—aligning our minds with God's mind, aligning our will with God's will, and aligning our emotions with God's emotions. The soul of **NOW** will affect your thinking process. It will affect His will, to be performed in and through you. Then submitting to His emotions to convict and control your emotions, in a beautiful way, so that you will know it's right at the bottom of your core being. The soul speaks in uniqueness, and **NOW** you are becoming that oneness in Christ as you move from Egypt through the desert and **NOW** abide in the Promised Land. Fear will try to set in, because there are giants in the land. We all must face the giants. If you do not have any giants in your life right **NOW**, you will from time to time. Do not run from your giants; it's time **NOW** for the David inside of you to stand up in your life and confront them one on one. Remember, Goliath had four brothers; that's why I think David had five smooth stones, just in case they decided to get in the fight that day. A giant just like David faced—after knocking him out with a stone, he cut his head off. Gee (gi), it was just an ant. Your "gi-ants" are just "ants"; it's only how you look at it if you are applying the **soul of NOW**. Trust God, and move at His pace for you as you conquer what God wants to connect your soul to. I hate to say it, but there are giants in the land—but let them be stepping-stones to your purpose and destiny. Looking at the soul of **NOW**, the giants are just a mere test, trying to stop you.

Gee it's Just A   **Gi - ant**

The soul of **NOW** has a place in God for you to travel with liberty, being sold out for the cause of Christ. This means being fully committed. We say we love God and serve Jesus, but our soul must line up with the Word of God. Taking it a step further, we must understand that this walk lies in the king and priest anointing talked about in book of Revelation. We have the authority to be ruling and reigning by His Spirit in our daily lives, keeping the soul intact, with everything going on. Today's kings are today's businessmen and women. Today's priests are todays ministers. Your talents and anointing may be stronger in business, or maybe in ministry, but we must understand our purpose, talents, and anointing in the soul. Do you see the trouble today—that so many businesses are not run with kingdom principles, and churches are trying to build their own kingdoms? Stop right here: prayer time—if we could get the business owners to work with the pastors, and the pastors to work with the business owners to break that generational curse, the world would be such a better place. Our communities, towns, cities, states, country, and world would be changed. The first type of businessman was Cain, who inherited a business plan from Adam to be a tiller of the ground. The first type of priest was Abel, a keeper of the sheep. We all know what happened: Cain killed Abel over an offering (money). Why are the "Cains" (business owners) and the "Abels" (priests/pastors/ministers) still fighting over money? Tell me if I am wrong: A true kingdom business owner should give ten percent of the profit to a local church/ministry, then pay employees, bills, and everything else. If that happened, and the members of our local churches paid tithes, our local church would have enough money to do whatever God told them to do. I know I am dreaming, because even a lot of Christian business owners do not operate in a kingdom-minded way, and we know that only about fifteen percent of members across the board tithe. Our soul of **NOW** has been robbed, but it can be changed by you—one person at a time.

Cain and Able

SPIRIT

3) The Spirit of NOW

The spirit of **NOW** is the heart of God, expressed through individuals who are living in the **NOW**. The spirit of man is the most inner part of how God made us. The Holy Spirit is awakened when we are born again. We should be led by the Spirit; and it also applies to the light within, knowing that we can be in the **NOW** by the Spirit, hearing from God. Walking daily in the **NOW** with God, doing His will by the power of His Spirit aligned with our spirit, flowing in what we call life. "If I ascend up into

heaven, thou art t........ .... ,
hold, thou art there" (Psalm 139:8 KJV). **NOW** can be
exercised like turning on a light switch. The sad thing
is that the Spirit (Holy Spirit) of the Trinity is the least
communicated with throughout the Body of Christ.
It's like the third verse in the Baptist hymn book when
it has four verses—it's hardly ever sung. It is also like
a car: if the car had three cylinders, the car would not
run smoothly if we only used two of them. If we do not
understand that we are three parts—body, soul, and
spirit—we will run rough. I know this is talking about
identity, but do believers understand that we are spirits, housed in a body with a soul? We call upon God,
and we call upon Jesus, but very few talk to the Holy
Spirit. The Holy Spirit is our Comforter, the One who
has been quickened and abides in us. When we die, our
spirit lives forever; we go to heaven or hell, depending
on how we applied Jesus, the Son of God. The Spirit of
NOW is connecting us to the Trinity of the Holy Spirit,
so **NOW** you are breathing the Father, Son, and Holy
Ghost (Holy Spirit). The third dimension of the **NOW**
is operating on all three cylinders of the body, soul, and
spirit.

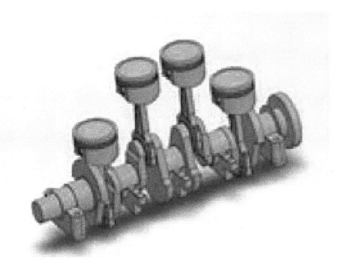

To have the right vision, purpose, attitude, prayer, passion, faith, peace, identity, power, victory, healing and revival you got to have the right tools.

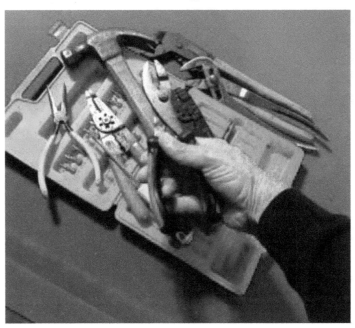

CHAPTER 3

The 12 Principles of NOW

The vision, purpose, attitude, prayer, passion, faith, peace, identity, power, victory, healing, and revival of NOW

1) The Vision of NOW

The vision of **NOW** is the defining moment when God gives you sight to begin your journey as a special visionary. Without a vision, the people perish. It takes seeing it before you can be it. Visualize things happing for you **NOW**. It's not time now to put on the brakes; it's time **NOW** to walk it, talk it, and expect it. What is your "it"? Visualize it and cast the vision; put it into the atmosphere with prayer and fasting. Be real about your dream. The Bible says, "Cast your bread upon the waters" (Ecclesiastes 11:1 NKJV). Habakkuk 2:2 (NIV) says, "Write the vision... so that [they] may run with it." If your vision is not bigger than you, it's not a true vision from God. Collect your thoughts, process your strategy, fix your mind and heart, and birth your vision **NOW**.

2) The Purpose of NOW

The purpose of **NOW** is one of the foundations to cement in your thoughts that answers the why, how, where, and when questions. **NOW** is the time, **NOW** is the place, and **NOW** is the reason to move into the purpose of doing God's will. God has placed you on this earth to fulfill His purpose through you **NOW**. Why me? How do I plan? Where do I begin? When will I finish? These are a few of the questions we ask God. Yes, God, my purpose is **NOW**. His purpose will line up with your plans. The purpose of His plan is drawn to your plans, the purpose of His goal is current with your goals, the purpose of His **NOW** is working with your **NOW**. A purposed mind, heart, and will makes a three-strand cord hard to break. Be still and know that God will give you purpose **NOW**!

3) The Attitude of NOW

The attitude of **NOW** is having the right mindset. The power to set the atmosphere by having the right attitude will accomplish it **NOW**. There is a positive and a negative side of attitude. If you say attitude slowly, it could sound like this: "add to you"; so, whatever you add to you, whether it's positive or negative, it sticks. Having the right outlook, with your expectancy turned up, will help to set the **NOW** things in place to acquire what you need. Allow your **NOW** attitude to add everything you need, suddenly and quickly, by having your mind focused on the **NOW** attitude. The **NOW** attitude plays a big part in the success of everything you do. A wholesome attitude sets the stage for the show to begin. Have you ever been at a play, and the lighting, music, and sound equipment were not right? That's the way it is: by having the wrong attitude, you will attract bad things to you, and things will not be right. So, let's fix the problem before it starts and walk in the attitude of **NOW** with gladness.

4) The Prayer of NOW

The prayer of **NOW** is putting your heart before God. Prayer is the key to hope, trust, and love. The second, third, and fourth letters of "prayer" spell ray—I call it the ray of hope. So, when you pray **NOW**, it sends a ray of hope to the person, place, or thing that you are declaring. We all know the importance of prayer, but you have to understand that we are prayer. This is what I mean by that: in the body, we come together to pray corporately; then we come in the soul to get the mind, will, and emotions of God as to what to pray about. Then in the spirit, we must understand that we are prayer. We are the answer to someone's prayer, or someone is the answer to our prayer. The prayer of **NOW** is in season every day to breathe the breath of God over everything. The prayer of **NOW** is walking, talking, listening, and thinking of God in every moment throughout a given day. When? **NOW**.

5) The Passion of NOW

The passion of **NOW** is the excitement of doing what you are passionate about. Going for it **NOW**. It's what you were made to do. So many of us, because of the responsibilities of life, run down the rabbit trail of working jobs just for the money to pay our bills, and we get tied down in the busyness of life and lose our way. So, the passion of **NOW** is to help and guide us with strength to accomplish the **NOW**. If we stay on the course and lay down the bricks one at a time, the wall or building will be built by our passion. So, ask yourself: what is your passion? If money was not the object, and you could do anything in the world with no limits, what would be your passion? Look at the **NOW**, and examine your roadblocks. What will it take to move them one at a time, to clear the road that few travel? Do not just quit your job and go for broke; use wisdom in your decision making. Plan your passion, prepare your passion, and play your passion **NOW**. Have fun with your journey until you finally arrive. Grow with the experiences on the way. The passion of **NOW** is a passing—saying goodbye to the past and hello to the future. You are passing the lessons, learning each step of the way, meeting different people, and proving something to yourself every day. What a blessing it is to find your passion and share it with others along the way.

6) The Faith of NOW

The faith of **NOW** is a foundation piece that cannot waver. We know that we all have been given or dealt a measure of faith. This happened at the day of salvation, so let's connect our faith with Jesus' faith and use His faith **NOW**. No more waiting or wavering faith, but ultimate faith, following the guidance of the Holy Spirit. Faith is an action word, and **NOW** is also, so when you put them together it makes you act on them **NOW**. Just imagine, when two anointed people work together for kingdom purpose, how much stronger they are than just one working alone. In the Body of Christ, we see a lot of ministries building their kingdoms. What would happen if pastors and ministries would join together in one accord more than we see today? I wonder, would it make a difference in the world? Surely it would if we could all just get along, working together for the cause of Christ and His kingdom. If the different denominations would lay down their differences and work together for the cause of Christ in our communities, the world would be a much better place. If Jesus was really our focus, and we would not split hairs over every doctrine and belief, I believe we would see revival spread so much faster. The faith of **NOW** needs to flow in government, business, and the church. God ordained three institutions: the home, the church, and the government. Everything starts at home. If the home were right, the church would be right. The church is messed up because the home is jacked up. So, the folks who put people in government are messed up because it started at home and went through the church, and we wonder why government is not what it should be. The faith of **NOW** will help the home, church, and government. So, where is your faith **NOW**? I hope that this challenges you to break every generational curse over you and your family. With this in mind, let faith run its course **NOW**, in every area of life.

HOME

CHURCH

7) The Peace of NOW

The peace of **NOW** is simply the grace of knowing that you are doing the right thing. The peace of God surrounds you every second of the **NOW**. Outside of love, peace is the next greatest need we have; and with the anointed peace and the will of God, there is no other place I would rather be. Just taking every breath, breathing in the peace of God, is the best atmosphere that could be established and set to operate in. The question is, how many times do we do things without having the peace of God? In the **NOW** moments of your life, fill them with the peace of God **NOW**. He will do it for you. The peace of **NOW** is the best highway you could travel. If you do not have peace, begin asking the Peacemaker to come quickly and watch the hand of God restore, redeem, and resurrect. The peace of **NOW** is a treasure, the gift of being in the center of God's will. Sometimes it's like you are in the eye of a tornado with things flying all around you, but you have peace in the midst of the storm. Peace can be costly—giving up everything you have and leaving it all in God's hands to handle. Then at the appointed time, He returns greater to you, so much that it will blow your mind. It's a give-and-take relationship called the process of God. The peace of **NOW** is simple or complex, depending on how you want to look at it. The bottom line is: choose peace **NOW**.

8) The Identity of NOW

The identity of **NOW** is identifying what is your **NOW**. It is the true identity of who you are in Christ, applying the anointing of God and understanding what to do in the present moment. It is so important that we find that identifying purpose of what to do, when to do it, and where to do it. So, do not be afraid to ask God questions. In identifying who, what, where, and when questions, it helps to develop a clear thinking process to discover every time the **NOW** factor needs to be applied. Identity is the key to unlocking door after door of success. Failure is a building tool to step out and find the identity of your **NOW**; search for it like a hidden treasure. The treasure is you. Knowing the identity of the **NOW** unlocks gates, doors, and secret pathways of everything you desire and need. Ask yourself this question: Are you knocking on the right doors? Find the truth, seek wisdom, and fulfill your quest. Everybody tries to identify themselves through family, careers, and relationships, but our true identity lies in Jesus Christ. For years, I did not know what "in Christ" meant. The identity of **NOW** is so important in order to have a complete understanding of how to handle your success when it is **NOW**.

9) The Power of NOW

The power of **NOW** sets time limits, knowing that you are carrying a bomb of blessings to blow the world up with the goodness that has been stored in you since before you were born. God loads you up daily with benefits, and He knows the plans He has for you. You are so powerful, and equipped for greatness. The power of **NOW** is also a unique understanding of your strength, ready to be used at the drop of a hat when needed. Dynamite power (*dunamis* in the Greek): to change the present with the anointing grace that is in us through Jesus Christ. The power of **NOW** is an open door of opportunity to set things in motion, and to keep things moving from the spirit world to the natural world. Working together causes the supernatural to work faster and stronger. So, put your explosives in place, causing a supernatural effect to blast your way into your purposed destiny. Realize the power that you have through Jesus Christ, and His anointing that abides in you. The power of **NOW** is just waiting for you to press the button.

10) The Victory of NOW

The victory of the **NOW** is an attitude: knowing that no matter where you are—in the valley, on the mountain, or going through—you have the victory. Even if you look like you are losing, the victory of **NOW** is a boldness of determination that no matter what happens, you have already won. If God is for us, who can be against us? (Romans 8:31). Even if there are giants facing you, you can have the spirit of David and apply the Word of God and claim your victory. So many

Christians live in defeat, but with the victory of **NOW** attached to you, you are an overcomer—when? **NOW**!

11) The Healing of NOW

The healing of **NOW** is necessary to apply with any type of pain or disorder you have. We are healed **NOW**—not yesterday, but **NOW**. Take any kind of sickness: let's say you have been to the doctor and you were given a diagnosis. Listen to the doctor; God uses science and doctors, but God has the final say-so. I believe in the supernatural healing of Jesus Christ, the One who created me and is in charge of my life. Pain in your body is not for you! The pain is for you to intercede for the Body of Christ, or individuals that the Holy Spirit shows you. After you pray, tell that pain or sickness to get off your body, **NOW**. Healing is a process, so there may be a delay **NOW**, but a miracle is right-away healing. There again, we've got to open up our mouths and speak away pain, disorders, bad relationships, bad emotions, thoughts, whatever is attacking us, **NOW**. The healing of **NOW** is a tool we cannot leave in our toolbox. You are healed; your mind is right; your body is aligning to total health. I speak life, not death, to you **NOW**.

12) The Revival of NOW

The revival of **NOW** is a revealing of the underlying purpose of what needs to take place in your life. Crawl, walk, or run with the revival Spirit of operating in the **NOW**. Let your movement be real and begin suddenly. Revival is here; take your place and be rejuvenated and revived, taking dominion. There is a wind coming from the North, South, East and West—a wind of revival, just for you. So, it's time **NOW** to set your sail and let the wind of the Holy Ghost blow on your relationships, business, and ministry. God is willing; are you? Check the old landmarks, broaden your borders, and extend your tents for the revival of **NOW**, for God to move at will. You have been chosen—a special, sent one for your task. Millions are counting on you. You are worthy. So, revive your dreams, revisit your vision, and accept your personal revival of **NOW**.

CHAPTER 4

The 12 Confessions of NOW

Confess with your mouth and believe with your heart; there is a truth about confessions that bring about change by putting words into the atmosphere. Speak these confessions of **NOW** over your life every day, to see the true person you are **NOW**.

1. God, I thank You for the vision You have given me **NOW**, continually, to help me see clearly all the visions and dreams that You want me to fulfill **NOW**, that my legacy will be established **NOW**.

2. Lord, I speak Your purpose in and through me **NOW**, calling destiny to line up with my purpose, **NOW** and forevermore. I will serve Your purpose **NOW**.

3. Jesus, set my attitude **NOW**, with all humbleness and with confidence bringing a divine balance **NOW**, in the physical and spiritual realm **NOW**. My attitude is set **NOW** by the anointing of God.

4. I declare that I am prayer **NOW**; I walk in the spirit of prayer, being a ray of hope in every situation **NOW**. I pray Your grace upon my life **NOW**.

5. My passion grows deeper **NOW** as I think on the goodness of God; my love and devotion are overflowing **NOW**. My passion is fulfilled **NOW**.

6. I stand true to my faith **NOW**, trusting the Holy Spirit to guide my footsteps to advance the kingdom of God **NOW**. I connect my faith to Jesus' faith **NOW**.

7. I choose to live in peace **NOW**. Peace is all about me; no matter what I face, peace rests in me **NOW**. Every breath I take is a **NOW** peace.

8. I identify the identity that is connected to Christ **NOW**. My identity in Christ is who I am **NOW**. Identity is one of my keys to success **NOW**.

9. The ultimate power of God controls me **NOW**. Power is one of my spiritual vitamins that I take **NOW**. I receive the power of **NOW** over my life **NOW**, to have the strength to overcome.

10. Victory belongs to me **NOW**. I live in the victory that overcomes the world **NOW**. I am a winner

at all costs **NOW**. Every situation in my life bows down to my victory **NOW**.

11. I am healed **NOW** by the blood of Jesus. I speak to my healing **NOW**, that every situation—whether in my body, soul, or spirit—lines up and resolves **NOW**.

12. I receive revival **NOW** in every area of my life. Revival is here **NOW**. The season of revival has come **NOW**. **NOW**, I speak revival to dead situations that need resurrection **NOW**.

CHAPTER 5

OWN

The OWN Factor:
Principle of Taking Ownership without
Possessing It Yet

The **OWN** Factor is taking ownership, just like you already have it. We must speak and declare the things that God has already ordained and prepared for us. Proverbs 18:21 (NKJV) says: "Death and life are in the power of the tongue." One of the main things that we must learn to control is our tongue, in order to speak, believe, and have whatever we say. I have broken down the word tongue for a better understanding: *ton / gue = when we speak*, it's a ton of glue without the l. So, whether our words are positive or negative, our words will stick. Our words can build up and encourage, or tear down and destroy. The **OWN** factor is a principle to speak things until they manifest. It is connecting the spiritual to the physical. We should write it, speak it, and rejoice like we have already received it by the grace of God. **OWN** it, whatever your "it" is.

The Three (3) Dimensions of OWN

3D

God made man with three parts: body, soul and spirit. Let's look at the **OWN** in body, soul and spirit.

1) The Body of OWN

The Body of **OWN** is a confident look which is reflected in your face, your body posture, and even your walk. Think about how you would act, knowing that you **OWN** something of great value—the confidence of knowing it belongs to you. In other words, your whole demeanor and body language would change, and others would understand that you are completely in control of what you have. In refereeing, you have umpires or officials that have a chip on their shoulder that they know the rules, inside and out. They are in control, and you cannot tell them anything. Sure, you need to keep the game in control, but be approachable by the coach. In your walk, **OWN** that godly control; make sure you show it, not with pride, but with humility. Your body is in shape to handle it with no problem. You have exercised for the moment. It's your time and your turn to carry it all the way. The body of **OWN** is an act of one's will lining up with God's plan, even when no one else understands. The control of God is placed in your hands, to make the right choices using your physical strength. **OWN** it **NOW** in your body, because you have the tools.

2) The Soul of OWN

The soul of **OWN** is lined up in your mind, will, and emotions. Your mind is set, your will is in tune, and your emotions will demonstrate and show that you will attain what you strive for, because you already have it. Nothing can change your mind, will, and emotions. Your soul is sold out in such a positive way that others step back, because they see that you have it. The soul is surrounded by your passion. Your heart is beating so strongly, and nothing can stop you. You have been taking baby steps, but **NOW** it's time to start taking giant steps. The soul of **OWN** truly helps you to dig deep within your mind, will, and emotions to have the right thinking. It directs your will to line up with your purpose.

This is where you allow the Holy Spirit to tap into God's will for your life, and when the two agree—your will and God's will—it makes a perfect force to **OWN**. Your emotions can throw your mind and will off. So, balance is the key to use to unlock every door. Emotions play a big part in working with your mind and will.

OWN your soul by giving it back to God. Give Him your mind, will, and emotions to achieve the fullness that God has for you. The soul of **OWN**, in full operation, will cause you to move with power to **OWN** everything that God allows.

3) The Spirit of OWN

The spirit of **OWN** is set solid by every aspect that ties the body, soul, and spirit together in an absolute way that cannot and will not change. Having the spirit of **OWN** will bring about the final shape of **OWN**ing it. It will become a part of you as the right Spirit attaches with wisdom, understanding, and knowledge. The spirit of **OWN** is the root of obtaining **OWN**ership. The Holy Spirit that abides in us is our power source to **OWN**. Guidance by God through the Holy Spirit is a must. We **OWN** and attract what is in our spirit. I love to meet people who have the right spirit. It's those kinds of people whom I love to support, and I allow them to rub off on me. We live in a world with all kinds of spirits. It is spiritual warfare every day. So, that's why you want to protect your spirit in every area that you can. I'll say it this way: that's why I pray on the full armor of God every day. Putting on your spiritual clothes is as important, as you prepare for the day, as putting on your physical clothes. Your spirit of **OWN** will be pro-

tected, and you can move by His Spirit to get to your
Promised Land.

CHAPTER 6

The 12 Principles of OWN

The vision, purpose, attitude, prayer, passion, faith, peace, identity, power, victory, healing, and revival of OWN.

1) The Vision of OWN

The vision of **OWN** is taking **OWN**ership like you already have what you are striving for. You see it and believe that you **OWN** it. The vision is seeing it before you possess it. **OWN** your vision, see it for yourself, and operate in what you see. Others may see it before you, but you must be able to see it for yourself to **OWN** it. The vision of **OWN** gives you a circle of awareness, of foresight and hindsight. It gives you a clear picture that you see in your mind: that you already **OWN** what God wants you to have. Remember, a picture speaks louder than a thousand words. So, we must picture and imagine ourselves doing, getting, and being in a position to achieve everything that belongs to us. Visualization plays such a big role in accomplishing and achieving our desired goals of **OWN**ing that which we desire. **OWN** your vision, create your vision board, and write your confessions. When you are in agreement with God and begin to decree a thing, it opens the door to the supernatural. The Holy Ghost is a gentleman, but when you activate the Word it puts a demand on the Holy Spirit to give you the vision of **OWN**.

2) The Purpose of OWN

The purpose of **OWN** is a fulfillment of **OWN**ership. Possess the land and claim your promise. It's your purpose to **OWN** everything that God wants you to have. You have the deed; the title is yours. **OWN** your relationships, **OWN** your ministry, and **OWN** your business to fulfill your purpose. If we will just pause and be still, God can pour into us all that we need, and our purpose to **OWN** it all. Purpose is a (pur) pure / (pose) pose. The picture is already in the frame; hang it on the wall. The purpose of **OWN** answers the why. Why should you **OWN**? How will **OWN**ing it, or doing it, help fulfill your goals and purpose? The purpose of **OWN** is here **NOW**.

3) The Attitude of OWN

The attitude of **OWN** will be the statement settled in your mind. When you set the atmosphere of your mind, you will have a complete, clear, right attitude toward **OWN**ing everything that God has for you. **OWN** your attitude in such a way that it's no mistake that you will walk through every door with confidence in your heart and mind that you **OWN** it. The attitude of **OWN** is not just a concept; it should be a lifestyle. We should wake up proclaiming that it is going to be a great day with the attitude to **OWN** the day—not with the wrong type of pride, but the right humility. Say "Top of the morning" to get your attitude of **OWN** moving in the right direction. "This is the day the Lord has made" is a good way to have the right attitude started every day. It takes work. They say it takes twenty-one days to start or break a habit, but after you have worked hard to **OWN** it, it feels good to make it happen. Practice does not make perfect; it makes better.

4) The Prayer of OWN

The prayer of **OWN** is an on-time prayer. This anointing takes ownership of what you are praying for to another level. The prayer of **OWN** helps you to establish a new confidence—knowing that you will receive and get the answer to your prayer. **OWN** your prayer time. Do not be a wishy-washy kind of person when asking God for something; act like you already have your answer when you pray. There are two types of prayers: the first type is a selfish, doubtful, wishing prayer, and the other type is a bold, confident, on-point, believing, faith-full prayer, with a knowing that God will move on your behalf. **OWN** your soul right when you pray, and pray with

Jesus' faith and not your faith only. The prayer of **OWN** is yours, today and every day after this. The prayer of **OWN** is seeing the end even in the beginning of your prayer. This anointing also knows the direction you are going in your prayer. You and I **OWN** that prayer. Before I wrote this book, I knew that I **OWN**ed the words on these pages before I typed them out. I hope that you really understand the power that we have in this anointing to **OWN** our words of prayer. Prayer is also listening; even that is our right to **OWN** everything that is being said. The prayer of the **OWN** principal teaches us to govern our words, to declare ownership to the fullest extent. Taking ownership of your prayer makes all the difference in the world in understanding that you **OWN** it.

5) The Passion of OWN

The passion of **OWN** is having the excitement and zeal to **OWN** it. Let your passion be so strong that nothing will keep you from ownership. **OWN** your passion for whatever you want to do. Let your passion stand out; be devoted to your cause in such a way that there will be no mistaking which way you are going: to **OWN** it with passion. The passion of **OWN** is turning the power to another level and sowing into your future, with excitement and full of zeal. Get in the passing lane of your destiny and go your **OWN** speed limit. Live and breathe for your passion to **OWN** your passion. "Do" you! Does your game play hard as you **OWN** your **OWN** reward?

Success is born out of faith, an underlying passtion, and a relentless drive.

6) The Faith of OWN

The faith of **OWN** is a pillar that stands tall, to hold up the building and to make room for you to **OWN** what God has for you. Let Jesus' faith connect to your faith and know that you **OWN** it, thanking God in advance for **OWN**ing it. Faith will take you the distance to

OWN it without a shadow of a doubt. The faith of **OWN** is speaking, declaring, and knowing that it's going to happen. All we have to do is to exercise our belief system and get it into the shape to **OWN**. To exercise your faith, you must flex your spiritual muscles, and draw out your plans as if you were playing a game or building a building. We must grow from faith to faith, understanding our gifts and talents. **OWN** your faith, so you can cross every Jordan in your life.

7) The Peace of OWN

The peace of **OWN** comes with a complete understanding of who wants you to **OWN** and have the things you need. There is nothing like having the peace of God; and when applied, it's good knowing what belongs to you. Peace lines up with having the faith that you already **OWN**, so why worry? Walk in **OWN**ing all the peace that you need by His grace. The peace of **OWN** is the place of rest while you are moving. It's the place to restore, redeem, and reassure you that you can and will **OWN** it. I have been refereeing wrestling for over forty-five years for high school, and I have studied the wrestlers. In my findings, the best wrestlers actually rest while they are wrestling. Rest is in the middle of w(rest)ling. What do I mean by wrestlers resting while wrestling? They have this peace about them—a balance not to overdo it, but to go at a pace to finish strong, in order to balance their talent and ability across the mat. They **OWN** their opponent, working their moves with grace to get the victory. Master the peace of God to **OWN** your peace in everything you do. So, when you **OWN** your peace and know where it comes from, then you can **OWN** all you want, knowing that God has already lined it up for you.

8) The Identity of OWN

The identity of **OWN** is having no doubt that you **OWN** it. You have already identified what you need, so you begin the process of acquiring the desires of your heart. If you have to roleplay, roleplay until it becomes a reality. How does this work? You identify that you **OWN** whatever it is—for example, call it by name. If it does not have a name, give it a name. Call it forth and when possible, write it down, describe it in detail. If you have a plan, work the plan by taking every step. It starts with identifying it, putting words to it, because you **OWN** it. The identity of **OWN** is accepting your mark. Too many try to find their identity in what they do— their work, their vocation, and what they have. Your identity is not in what you **OWN**; it's in you and your true identity, which comes by identifying the you in Christ. It's who you are in Him; this is the true source of your **OWN** identity. So many are missing their identity, thinking that what they **OWN** identifies them by material wealth. So, **OWN** your identity by identifying your worth in Christ Jesus, trusting God and letting Him add to you. One of my favorite words is think. If you can think it and identify it, you are more likely to achieve it. Think about identifying it to **OWN** everything you need. **OWN** it in your mind and heart, write it down, and then you will **OWN** your identity by understanding who you are and what is yours.

Own Your Identity

9) The Power of OWN

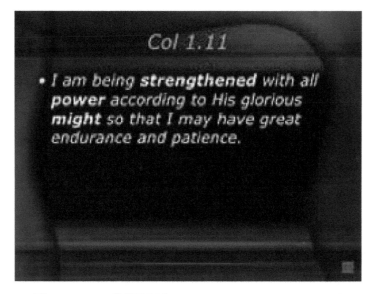

> Col 1.11
>
> • *I am being **strengthened** with all **power** according to His glorious **might** so that I may have great endurance and patience.*

The power of **OWN** knows your power source. One question you should ask yourself is: Does the all-powerful live in you? If He (Jesus, the Son of God) does, then that means you have the power pack, the power source already generated inside of you, to **OWN** whatever you want to **OWN**, in the twinkling of an eye. What assurance and confidence would you have, walking in the anointing of **OWN**? All we have to do is turn it on every morning. The power of **OWN** is a streamline of putting your faith to create the explosion of power. It's the force to set your mind and will to **OWN** whatever you desire. The power is the anointing. Talents and gifts are one thing, but when the anointed power is connected to it, nothing can stop it **NOW**. **OWN** the power that is freely given to you by Jesus Christ. Christ means "the Anointed One." So, when you are in Christ, you have the Anointed One inside of you to give you the power through Him for His glory to flow through you. This power to **OWN** is inside of you, waiting to be released anytime you need it. **OWN** your power every day.

10) The Victory of OWN

The victory of **OWN** is powerful in knowing that the battle to **OWN** is already over. We win; we have the victory to **OWN** every key to every door that God wants us to open, because He is the door. **OWN** your victory; dance your victory; dance before the first shot is fired. The victory belongs to us, because the battle is His. The victory of **OWN** is a measure and guidepost to work, fight, and overcome every battle. Sometimes when we lose, it's still a victory, because it releases tools to gather for the next battle or fight. Do not give up on your medal, trophy, or crown, because it is waiting for you. I know it's hard, but stand your ground and let the warrior arise within you to fight the good fight of faith and **OWN** your victory every day.

11) The Healing of OWN

The healing of **OWN** is yours totally, already in the bank of your spirit. "By His stripes you are healed" are not just words squeezed into the Bible, but words of ownership and life. That problem, pain, or disorder came from somewhere, but it does not need to stay. So, it works both ways—we **OWN** the right to remove or overtake whatever tries to mess with us. I know we age, and our body begins to break down, but God gives us spiritual and natural knowledge to share and **OWN** the methods to handle everything. So, we do not want to leave out the overcoming healing when we **OWN** His grace to apply the healing of **OWN**. We **OWN** the blood right of healing; we **OWN** the power of Christ to remove pain, disorders, or whatever is bothering us. For example: let's say the doctor says you have type 2 diabetes; okay, we turn on the anointing of **OWN** and find a game plan to make sure we have the right readings in our blood sugar, with the tools of wisdom and knowledge that we apply with the healing of **OWN**. We do not **OWN** diabetes; we allow the work process of **OWN** to regroup and fight and bring diabetes under control. **OWN** your healing today, by God's grace.

12) The Revival of OWN

The revival of **OWN** is revealing that you do **OWN** it. The reality is that you do have **OWN**ership. It's knowing that you've been given a body, soul, and spirit, and that you already possess it. Restored, redeemed, and revived adds up, because you dream it to be. Revival takes place because you have positioned yourself for change and transformation in order to receive. Too many people try to take **OWN**ership, but they do not count the cost. A building is finished because the **OWN**er counted the cost before the work began. Revival is here to **OWN** because you have counted the cost to submerge the event and project of your life in prayer. You will run into some obstacles along the way—surprises that you did not count on—but with the God factor in charge, your revival of **OWN** will stand strong as you stay humble in dealing with everything in the right way. Allow the God factor to revive your **OWN**.

CHAPTER 7

The 12 Confessions of OWN

God has so many desires for us, and many blessings. Life is not a bed of roses, but take these confessions and say them daily until they get down into your spirit, to help you understand that you already **OWN** all that God has for you.

1. I thank God for allowing me to **OWN** the vision that was birthed in me. Every true vision, I **OWN** now. I see what is before me, and I **OWN** the vision until the work is done.

2. I **OWN** the purpose that caught me by the grace of God. My purpose is **OWN**ed by God to show the world who I am. Purpose is in my **OWN** inner circle, where things are done in order.

3. I will **OWN** the right attitude as I add to others and show them how I **OWN** the gifts that God has given me. My attitude sets the stage for me to **OWN** and acquire what God has for me.

4. I connect to Jesus' spirit when I'm in prayer to **OWN** the words I speak; then I will carry out His works daily. I **OWN** my prayer with purpose every day.

5. My passion is **OWN**ed by God's desires for my every moment. **OWN**ing my passion is having the heart of God, so I **OWN** the heart of God. I have passion growing in me every day.

6. My faith that is connected to God shows that I **OWN** Jesus' faith, knowing the blueprints of His beliefs. I will carry out His will, as I **OWN** this right in Him. Jesus' faith is a tool that I exercise daily.

7. Understanding that I **OWN** the peace of God enables me to withstand the storms of life that come my way. I celebrate **OWN**ing the peace of each day. Peace is my attitude, a chosen fruit of the Spirit that I **OWN**.

8. The power I **OWN** is the power of the Word of God that I apply daily to my life. I **OWN** power over every decision I make, with guidance from the Holy Ghost. I love to walk in this power in my journey each day.

9. This moment, I **OWN** my identity in Christ, taking **OWN**ership of my worth as a human being. I **OWN** the God-given right of who I am. Identity is one of my prized possessions.

10. Before I begin, I **OWN** the victory and know the outcome will glorify the Lord. I **OWN** the victory through the whole process of whatever is going on in my life. I celebrate v-i-c-t-o-r-y now, as I **OWN** it.

11. I thank God in advance that I **OWN** my healing. I am healed in the name of Jesus Christ; no pain or problem has the right to stay. I **OWN** the healing that resides in me every day.

12. I prophesy and **OWN** revival in every relationship and situation for kingdom purpose. I am revival in the spirit of the word, helping others to find their destiny. The revival that I **OWN** changes everything for the better.

CHAPTER 8

WON

The WON Factor:
Principle of Winning and Walking in Victory

My senior year in high school, in 1977, I painted this picture in art class. The theme of the painting is: "Will Curtis Minter reach his goal in life?" Clarkston High School colors are green and gold, where I attended eleventh and twelfth grades. Lakeshore was light blue and red, where I was in eighth, ninth, and tenth grades. You can see that I am carrying the ball, and I am right at the goal line for the touchdown. The band is playing, the cheerleaders are cheering, the drill team is dancing, and the fans are going wild, waiting for me to cross the goal line for the winning touchdown. The defense is about to tackle me, but I believe and know that I will win, because I am living in the **WON** Factor.

The **WON** Factor is winning through life and having victories every day. This is a strong principle, with the knowledge that no matter what we are going through, we win in the end. Yes, we have **WON**, and we will continue to win. I understand that we may lose some battles along the way, but if you read the book of Revelation (the last book in the Bible), we are on the winning team no matter what we are doing. How good does it feel to know that you have **WON**? The fact that you are a winner, that you matter, and that you are not just a number means you are worthy in the eyes of God. Your worth is not based on what you do; it is based on who and whose you are. You are abiding in Christ, the One who rose on the third day, and you are walking in victory and all power. That same resurrection power that is in Christ is also in every believer. The grave could not hold Him; whatever happened in your past cannot hold you. **NOW**, take this principle and go change your generation.

The Three (3) Dimensions of WON

3D

1) The Body of WON

The body of **WON** understands physically that you have to exercise your muscles in preparation to win the fight or battle. Practice does not make perfect, but practice makes better, like I said before. The body of **WON** does not mean that you should be over-confident, but rather go through the physical stages to be a winner in the natural. When a game is **WON**, twenty percent (20%) is physical and eighty percent (80%) is mental, which adopts the process to gain the victory.

2) The Soul of WON

The soul of **WON** is getting the mind, will, and emotions set in place to picture the winning spirit. Wisdom plays a big part in having the understanding and the knowledge of God to apply to your heart and your soul, in order to come out on top. Also, balance is the key to keeping your mind, will, and emotions on a level playing field, and to jumping or getting around any hurdles or roadblocks that get in your way. You can move mountains if the soul of **WON** is balanced and your mind, will, and emotions are set for the task.

Mind - Will - Emotion
(Balance is the key)

3) The Spirit of WON

The spirit of **WON** is the root of the matter—to have the right Spirit, God's Spirit, to accomplish your goal, your dream, and your passion. When you turn on the spirit of **WON** every morning, your day will be so much brighter. Your path is lit for you to walk in obedience and righteousness, with the knowledge that you can do all things through Jesus Christ who strengthens you. Remember, you walk in His Spirit, and not yours alone. Greater is He that is in you than he that's in the world. The Spirit of **WON** is the fire that will burn until the job is done.

WALKING IN THE SPIRIT
Galatians 5:16

CHAPTER 9

The 12 Principles of WON

The vision, purpose, attitude, prayer, passion, faith, peace, identity, power, victory, healing, and revival of WON

1) The Vision of WON

The vision of **WON** is seeing the battle come to a complete victory, because we have **WON** the battle before the fight even begins. See yourself at the finish line; see yourself standing on the victory stand. Envision yourself going through the process of what it takes to win. Understand the power of your sight to see change and hope take place, because He who sees all is inside of you.

2) The Purpose of WON

The purpose of **WON** is taking your rightful destiny, where you can fulfill your purpose and win in the end. So, why not purpose to win every day? Learn to celebrate your identity in your purpose, because you are a winner. Even failing is a part of your purpose to win, because it places you in the column as the victor. Whenever you hear of someone who has played in a game, whether it was recreational or professional, the bottom line that people want to know is: "Who **WON**?" Oftentimes, if they did not get to see the game, the only thing they want to know is: "Who **WON**?" Did you win? Our purpose should be to win, but we cannot win every time, whether it's in a game or just in life. We know that favor is not fair. This is a dog-eat-dog world, and understanding that we must purpose to win is key. The purpose of **WON** is also not winning at everything we step out to do. Remember, it is a process, to shape and form us into what we should be. So, believe in yourself and purpose yourself; do what it takes to position yourself to be the best that you can be for the glory of God. I love to win when playing cards, checkers, basketball, or whatever I do, but I look for the lesson I'm to learn when I do not win, especially in the game of life. The purpose of **WON** is how you play the game. I referee and umpire small kids through college, and I am saddened when parents are so hard on their children when they lose. So many parents who coach their own children are reliving their own sports careers, and they make it too serious. They forget that it's just a game. Having the understanding of the purpose of **WON** will give you a destiny boost to propel you in your journey.

3) The Attitude of WON

The attitude of **WON** is a mindset to establish your victory. Having the attitude of **WON** is a major outlook and up-look toward success. If you think you can, you will. The right attitude will cause you to win through every process. Truth and control of your attitude plays a big part in **NOW**, **OWN**, and **WON**. Add the victory to your attitude and you will always come out on top. Attitude is one of the major keys to put you ahead of the crowd. The crowd is coming, and the crowd is doing their thing, so why not you? Adjust your attitude to be positive; your spirit will be on fire, so that when others come into your presence it will rub off on them to change their direction and outlook on life. This reminds me of when I was in the eleventh grade, having to take a history class that it seemed everybody hated. We had one of those teachers that the students talked about because she was tough as nails. So, I had heard all this stuff about her and the class. However, instead of conforming to what I had heard about the teacher and her history class, I purposed to have a great and good attitude and a positive outlook in the class. My posture was like a determined bulldog. I was going to hang on and do my very best. I believe that God positioned me right beside Laney. He was the most complaining, grumbling, miserable classmate I ever came across. On the first day of class, our teacher started laying on the homework big time, worksheet after worksheet. You could hear the complaints all across the room. So, to make a long story short, I spoke up and asked for more homework and more worksheets. By that statement, the teacher thought I was being a smart aleck, but God knew my heart. I just was having a super right attitude and being focused on staying ahead. So, she gave me more worksheets for punishment. But day after day, I entered my history class with a winning attitude. Ultimately, our teacher stopped giving me as much work as she gave to the other students. I was determined to have a great, good, and positive attitude in that class. Subsequently, it rubbed off on Laney and spread throughout the entire class. After it was all done and said, the teacher told me that because of my wonderful attitude and how it had spread throughout the entire class, our history class was the most enjoyable class she had ever taught. At that point in my life, I really did not know what I was doing. All I wanted was to survive my history class. However, God used me to change an entire history class. You can see how our attitudes can really make a difference.

4) The Passion of WON

The passion of **WON** is expecting, celebrating with your emotions, knowing and establishing the results. Release your passion to line up for victory. Make your passion to be a mandatory weapon for the battle. Take every ounce of your passion and focus on making it your cause, and you will already have **WON** the battle before it happens. Controlling your passion is a choice that you can measure your success with. The passion of **WON** is a powerful tool to take things apart and put things back together again. Work on your passion, knowing you have **WON**. You are a winner before you even start. Let the anointing flow like a river to get you down the stream of life. The passion is that driving force for success in whatever you do. However, the bottom line is that you must want to win—so let your passion guide you to victory.

5) The Prayer of WON

The prayer of **WON** takes time to develop. This is not a drawn-out, long prayer with long words and adjectives, but straight to the point, with an attitude, knowing it is done with a **BAM**: **B**lessings **A**nd **M**iracles. Prayer is a winning tool, for starters anyway, but we need to understand the anointing of the prayer of **WON** meaning—because my Christians are praying a lot of prayers but without purpose, power, and this kind of anointing for knowing they have **WON**. When I was a young teenager, I started praying for a ten-speed bicycle. I prayed strong for two weeks, and after fourteen days I stopped; on the fifteenth day my dad brought home a yellow, nice ten-speed bike. I was ashamed before God because I gave up; I did not believe that He was going to answer my prayer, but I learned that day to never give up—the prayer of **WON** works. I cannot tell you the many times—knowing that we have the authority over the weather—that it was raining cats and dogs right before my crew was having to referee a football game, and I would stick my arm out of the locker room with the rain soaking my arm with water, and I would pray the prayer of **WON** and ask God to hold off the rain while we refereed the game. In matter of seconds the rain would stop on a dime, and the guys on my crew would look at me really strangely. We have **WON** with our prayers.

6) The Faith of WON

The faith of **WON** is applying the true faith to win. Faith gives you the main tool, because you have already **WON**. It's not how you start, but it's how you finish. A sure faith will give you the victory and assurance that you have **WON**. Applying the faith of Jesus—knowing the score, the next move, or the next play before it happens—is the faith of **WON**. Have you ever seen a player or team that had the assurance and confidence that they were going to win? I grew up playing sports all the way through college, and the lessons I learned are unforgettable. There were times when I knew our team would do nothing and win hands down, but there were other times when I had no idea what the outcome would be. The faith of **WON** takes a strong belief system of core values, backed up by preparation. You are not going to win just because you show up. Your belief system must be right. Having the right faith, and using it at the right time, will cause powerful results to come in like a flood. I believe in using the faith of God as we pray, speak, or whatever we do. This will lead us to the **WON** column.

7) The Peace of WON

The peace of **WON** is having the peace of God, with no worries, in the entire process that God allows you to finish your task. Having the peace of God is the medicine to a successful journey. You have **WON** because He has already prepared the way for you to have your mind at peace. It is understood that love is the number-one need for human beings, and the second is peace. There is nothing like the peace of God—knowing in our heart and mind that we have **won**. It's like the sweetest artwork, framed for the canvas of our life. So many live today without the grace and merciful peace of God that is available. Every day is full of drama and turmoil. If you apply this principle of the peace of **WON**, you can start again and get back in the race you were created for. Run with deliverance, having the peace that you have already **WON**, over and over again. Having the peace of **WON** will get you from glory to glory, as the covering of God's mercy is on you. Then He will help you work through the rest with peace. It will also give you the confidence to rest through the war. We are in the seventh day of creation, and on the seventh day, God rested. The question is, does God get tired? No, but He rested to show us that we should rest after six days of work. If you understand biblical history, we are in the seventh day of the Lord, and we need to rest in our business, ministry, and relationships. If we could do it without having the peace of God, then it would be out of order and not the right relationship, business, or ministry. Let's talk about relationships for a minute, and how we should have the peace of knowing we have **WON** in our relationships, and how to flow with the peace of God. If peace is not in the relationship, that's a red flag of warning that needs to be taken care of. The same goes for business and ministry.

8) The Identity of WON

The identity of **WON** is completely seeing the big picture with your name in the victory column. This should be a process of discipline. Even though we know the battle and the ultimate victory are the Lord's, let's be mindful and do our part. Plan and create a strategy to win. Identify every detail it will take to rise to the top. Make your mark on the walls of history, leaving your legacy. The identity of **WON** is a standard reached in private, then executed at God's timing. As mentioned before, identity is the key. Imagine sitting in church, and around you, ninety percent of church folk don't know the fullness of who they are in Christ. Only ten percent of believers understand their purpose and identity. The Body of Christ is in an identity crisis. So, do you see the importance of coming into your identity of knowing that you have **WON**? Let's spread the message and help individuals come into their true identity, so we can walk in victory every day, understanding and knowing that we have **WON**. It's already been identified.

9) The Power of WON

The power of **WON** is the driving force to achieve victory. Like a car needs a battery, we need the Holy Spirit and the power of God not only to start us, but to carry us all the way to victory. If we did not have power—a drive to make it—we would be helpless. As we focus on the power of **WON**, we understand that we are entitled to victory. The power of **WON** is having the right kind of pride, surrounded with all we need, lacking nothing in Christ Jesus. The power of **WON** is also a powerful prayer life—one that talks to God and listens to what He tells us. The power also is given through the fruits of the Spirit and the gifts of the Spirit. The bottom line is knowing that you are powerful in Christ Jesus. Because He is a winner, it automatically makes us, the believers, powerful to win. The power of the **WON** principle enables us to claim victory before the game, battle, or war begins. Statistics state that before a game begins, eighty percent is mental and twenty percent is physical. Having the level of the power of **WON** puts us at the finish line long before the game begins.

10) The Victory of WON

The victory of **WON** is the assurance of accomplishment. The victory of **WON** is like a sweat-less victory. I am sure there will be times when you will have to sweat, but be assured that God will give you the victory. We win in the end; even though we may not be there yet, we are victorious. Go ahead and make your mark, because you have **WON**. The battle belongs to the Lord, so that's why you should pray on the armor of God every morning as you start your day. Just think about it—how many Christians go through the day without being spiritually dressed for the battle? A football player would not show up to a game without his pads on. A police officer would not start his duty without his uniform and gun. I have been praying on the armor of God for eighteen-plus years every day, and I can testify that it works. A true solider of Jesus Christ knows the principle of the victory of **WON** because he or she is dressed for the part. Victory is mine; victory is yours. Put on the armor of God and march, dance, and enjoy the victory of **WON**.

11) The Healing of WON

The healing of **WON**: it is very important to understand this anointing—that no matter what is thrown at you, no matter what the score is, you have **WON**. We have the total victory. Can you imagine knowing down in your gut, before you faced a problem or pain, or maybe a business deal, that you have **WON**? This is a lifestyle anointing to program in your mind. In eighth, ninth, and tenth grades I played football at Lakeshore High School in College Park, GA. For three years we did not lose a game. Most of the time we were up forty points before halftime, but the way we practiced and were coached, we had a confidence that we would win. We would line up and do our job, go through the process. It was a fact and a mindset; we had **WON** before the game started. With the healing of **WON**, the anointing does not lose. You win in your health, relationships, business, and ministry. I am so glad that we are on the winning team, with the powerful anointing of the healing of **WON**.

12) The Revival of WON

The revival of **WON** is making your mark of legacy. The victory has been revealed. You are the comeback kid. You could've been the underdog, but you are at the top of your game. It is a willingness to finish the race; the power of unstopping you; a force risen deep within. You have revealed what it takes to be in the winning channels of life. Run with your victory into another battle, to win another war. Let the revival of **WON** carry you to the next level, the next cause, and all the way into your destiny. The revival moment, mixed with the right ingredients, will help you overcome as you put your total trust in God. The stage is set, the time is right, and your homework is done. The world is yours; let the revival waves carry you the distance. The hope is shared, the trust is manifested, and the partners have arrived.

You are on a team, working as a unit to change the way people think and do things. The power that God has given you is in your hands. The revival of **WON** is your encouragement.

CHAPTER 10

The 12 Confessions of WON

Take these confessions and say them every day, to set your mind and heart to the anointing that you have already WON. We are winners; yes, we may lose a battle here or there, but though God we have **WON** the war.

1. The vision has been **WON** as I look through the eyes of God. I have **WON** the vision that was given to me, so I understand that I can win through the process. The vision has me, and I have the vision.

2. Here and now, I have **WON** because of the Jesus purpose that has been fulfilled and established in me. I am on the winning side of life. My purpose is great, and I am so glad that I have **WON**.

3. Before it starts, I have **WON**, because God has taught me to have the right attitude through life. I have **WON** with my outstanding attitude that I choose to possess with a sound mind—a winning attitude.

4. Confidence carries my prayer life to a different level, and it shows everyone that I have **WON**. Knowing this—that I have **WON**—changes everything. Prayer is my voice, talking and listening to God, knowing that I have **WON**.

5. The supernatural lifts my passion in the ways of the Lord. Doing this sets the laws of attraction in order, knowing this: I have **WON**. Knowing I have **WON** turns events in my favor, because my passion is right. My passion is full to bless others.

6. I have **WON** in my faith because I trust in God; my help comes from Him. My faith is the strongest when connected to Jesus; He is the reason I have **WON**. My winning faith takes me to the places where I need to go.

7. I love to walk in peace, knowing that I have **WON** before I even start. Peace is mine to hold and carry every day; my future is full of peace, because I have **WON**. Mercy plus grace equals peace is the equation that adds up to knowing I have **WON**.

8. I have a winning identity, because I know I have **WON** from the start to the finish. I am humble but confident, knowing I have **WON** with the grace that is on my life. Understanding my identity strengthens my character.

9. The power of **WON** is all over me in life, through the good and the bad. I walk in the power of **WON**, knowing that this anointing sets me on course every day to handle every task that comes my way. Power through Christ is the answer to my success.

10. Victory is my lifestyle, knowing that I have **WON** in every area of my life. I have **WON**, knowing that the battle belongs to the Lord—that's why I have **WON**. Victory comes from God, and He freely gives it to me.

11. By His stripes I am healed, trusting and knowing that I have **WON** and that everything has been through the healing process. I have **WON** in my healing through the power of Jesus Christ.

12. It is revival time in everything that I do, because I have **WON**. With God's help, every situation has been placed for revival NOW, knowing that I have OWNed it and that I have already **WON**, every time.

CHAPTER 11

Conclusion

The conclusion of **NOW**, **OWN**, and **WON** is the anointing that makes the difference. Walking, living, and determining to do it **NOW**, **OWN** it now, and know that we have already **WON**. So, just go through the process of what God has for you, with boldness to achieve your goal and dream with the passion that God has given you. **NOW**, **OWN**, and **WON** is the Tic-Tac-Toe of life that will help propel you into your destiny, giving you the principles and understanding to grow. Accept the anointing of **NOW**, **OWN**, and **WON** as you live, walk, and develop all that God has for you.

What about the **NOW**, **OWN**, and **WON** with positive and negative, good and evil? Positive and negative are in almost everything. Good versus evil is present in almost everything also, so God will use the bad for our good. Pressure does not feel good, but the pressure makes us better. Every movie has good and evil to make the story. From the very beginning, God created angels with free will. He knew that one angel named Lucifer, who was over worship, would fall; good and evil started in the world. Trials come left and right; the question is, will you pass the test when bad comes knocking at your door? We fight the fight of faith at every hand. We must turn on the anointing of **NOW**, **OWN**, and **WON**. We can handle the negative trials and know we can handle it **NOW**. On the reverse, we do not **OWN** the affliction—we take the test and show that we do not **OWN** the evil; we send it back to hell where it came from. That's why we have **WON**; even when the score or situation is upside down, we can turn it right side up and step into the winning circle with a positive attitude, with confidence, playing the victory song.

I wonder in the Bible stories if Abraham, Moses, David, Daniel, and so many more understood the trials and enemies they had to face; if they knew the Tic-Tac-Toe of Life, understanding that they acted **NOW**, had the attitude of **OWN**, and had the confidence that in the end they had **WON**. Yes, the winning team had already **WON** before the conflict, the battle, had even started.

Even looking at the *Tic-Tac-Toe* of Life: as we think about it, time is "*Tic*-ing" away; that's why we need to step into the **NOW, NOW!** There are things we need to "*Tac*" down and accomplish it to **OWN** it. If we walk in the **WON** anointing, we will "*Toe*" and carry the things that are needed in our life, or remove them. We must "*Toe*" and transport things along the way to build the path of our journey.

The **NOW**, **OWN**, and **WON** anointing is like a three-strand cord, hardly broken, and a trinity to work together. It reminds me of a three-cycle engine running in sync, functioning all together, smoothly. Just like a believer in Christ, we are made in His image, operating in balance, functioning and taking care of the body, soul, and spirit, well-rounded and used for the glory of God.

NOW is the time; **OWN** it is the attitude; and **WON** is the victory dance. The *Tic-Tac-Toe* of Life is a three-in-a-row anointing; **NOW**, **OWN**, and **WON** should be your daily vitamins. So, take this authority and play the game of life, and you will see that by taking these words you have learned to heart, they will change your life like they have mine. Go through the process that you can have it **NOW**, you can **OWN** it, and you have **WON**. Anointing is like attitude—it's everything. Can you imagine reaching all of your goals, dreams, and visions in a matter of time—having the mindset with sure confidence, knowing that you can achieve your heart's desire? I have good news: you can. The **NOW**, **OWN**, and **WON** principles are all in order for you in this book. Put **NOW**, **OWN**, and **WON** in action today to change your life and your world. It's a simple perspective of really walking in the things that God desires for you and others, so share this book with family and friends to change one life at a time.

Turn on your **NOW**, walk in your **OWN**, and remember that you have **WON**. I know you will never look at **NOW**, **OWN**, and **WON** the same ever again, and thank you for believing enough in me to read this book. God bless you.

Tic-Tac-Toe—yes, three in a row. It's time as the clock ticks away that we get moving to do the things that God has for us. To take every hour, every minute, and every second to nail down our gifts and talents for God to use us mightily. Be a kingdom builder. Let's *"Toe"* in all the blessings and give ourselves back to God to be used in any way He desires.

Tic-Tac-Toe is the timing, talent, and treasure that are in you to be used for kingdom purposes. As we get a *"Toe"* hold and *"Tac"* by tacking every promise down, and watch the clock of God *"Tic,"* time will be on our side. Strangely enough, we are in the cycle of life—we played ***Tic-Tac-Toe*** in school, and now as we grow into adulthood, we are still playing the game, but in a different light.

NOW, **OWN**, and **WON** is our game; **NOW**, work all three words with the anointing principles behind them for life. We can find a good example of the **NOW**, **OWN**, and **WON** anointing in the Word of God in Luke 18:1-9, the parable of the widow woman. She needed help **NOW**, and the wicked judge was the only one who could help her. By her continually coming to the judge, she **OWN**ed her answer before the judge gave in. She knew she had already **WON** the situation, but she had to go through the process. So, after her continually coming, the wicked judge said to himself, "Does not God avenge his **OWN** speedily?" (v. 8). Her mind was set to operate in the **NOW**, **OWN**, and **WON** anointing to get the problem solved. So, it's time to fly. Come off the diving board of life like I did in this picture, trusting that you will land right.

The choice is yours—let the process of God guide you **NOW**. **NOW** is the time to be inspired for greatness. **OWN** your destiny day by day. You have **WON**; victory has already been decided. I see your name in the winning column. The question is: Are you going to do it **NOW**? Do you see how you already **OWN** it? And do you see and know that you have already **WON**? *Tic-Tac-Toe*, three in a row. The **NOW**, **OWN**, and **WON** anointing is yours—when? **NOW!**

CHAPTER 12

Definitions

Let's break it down one more time, spiritually, in the third dimension. I call these definitions rightly dividing the Word:

Vision = a vice to handle issues seen and unseen to achieve the victory. Go through the valleys of life having the vision, seeing yourself on the other side. We have to see it before we can be it. Write the vision; write down what you see yourself achieving. Without vision, the people perish. The more you see, the more you will accomplish.

Purpose = (pur/pose): pose and be still, and then you will see (se) God pour (po) into you, and when He pours (po) into you, then He will position (pos) you. We know it's a dog-eat-dog world in the corporate world, and a power/title fight in the church world to gain position. If for some reason someone gets into that position with wrong motives, it will not last, but when God positions (pos) you, it is very positive (pos), like a cross and a plus sign (+). So, through the process, keep yourself pure (pur); if you mess up, repurify yourself. So, a pure (pur) pose (pose)—a pure pose—gives you a divine (p u r p o s e); a divine, pure pose gives a divine *purpose*.

Attitude = attitude can be positive or negative. Say it slowly, and it could sound like this: "add to you." When you add the wrong things, they stick. When you add good things, they stick. So, attitude is a choice where we choose to be positive or negative. Having the right attitude changes your atmosphere.

Passion = passion can be said like this: "pass it on"; so, we need the right kind of passion through the Son (Jesus). We need to lose our life and find our life in Jesus Christ; that's how to have His passion pass on to us.

Prayer = p (ray) er: "ray" is right in the middle of prayer. So, when you pray or someone prays for you, it shines a ray of hope on you or the person you are praying for.

Faith = fa (it) h: what is your "it"? Faith will take you as far as you want to go. Take the "it"—the very thing you are most passionate about—and attach it to Jesus' faith, and experience the power.

Peace = peace is a place. It is a start, like the vegetable (pea), that is good to the taste. Peace is an ace of perfection that God gives us.

Identity = God wants to put a "dent" into us, where we will be identified in and through us by His mark. So, our ID, our identity, defines who we are. There again, we must find that "it." The "it"—what we do, our purpose—is not to get mixed up with who we are—our identity—but we long to live out our purpose with true passion that drives us up and down the path of life.

Power = power is the "pow" of wisdom, weaved for strength for the believer to choose at any time. True power comes from the Holy Spirit that abides in us, so let the wind of eternity carry you through every grace and mercy of God, with power.

Victory = is the vice grip to take and unlock the territory of your life. Since the battle is His, all we have to do is go through the process and claim the war. The valleys may be low, but the mountains are high, so tell your story of how you attained victory.

Healing = healing is an "aligning" of whatever is out of order, and it's God almighty (He) who uses people to speak it. Healing is a process, so that's why we claim it.

Revival = a revealing of a new covering of His revival Spirit, with a vital message for all God is doing in this season. It is placing a new veil on the Body of Christ to be redeemed as His bride, the church. Revival is a re-birth of one's spirit to line up with the Father's will and carry out His plans.

Word Puzzle

(A word search puzzle with the
main words used in the book.)

```
k  q  c  v  p  a  s  s  i  o  n  d  h
u  f  a  i  t  h  z  s  q  b  a  y  e
w  e  t  s  n  o  j  o  r  e  n  r  a
p  c  t  i  o  w  n  u  e  y  o  o  l
r  a  i  o  w  o  n  l  w  z  i  t  i
a  e  t  n  b  o  d  y  o  j  n  c  n
y  p  u  r  p  o  s  e  p  t  t  i  g
e  i  i  d  e  n  t  i  t  y  i  v  o
r  n  d  s  p  i  r  i  t  n  n  c  d
m  z  e  t  o  e  l  o  v  e  g  l  x
```

now faith power passion own pin
attitude peace soul anointing tac
identity purpose body victory tic
won spirit prayer love vision toe
wuk healing obey god

Key to Word Puzzle

```
k q c v p a s s i o n d h
u f a i t h z s q b a y e
w e t s n o j o r e n r a
p c t i o w n u e y o o l
r a i o w o n l w z i t i
a e t n b o d y o j n c n
y p u r p o s e p t t i g
e i i d e n t i t y i v o
r n d s p i r i t n n c d
m z e t o e l o v e g l x
```

Contact information: *www.power-in-names.com*

The End

(For right NOW)